A Brief History
of Barge Poles

Keith Pepperell

DEDICATION

To my spawn Jack, Lydia, and Alex none of whom have ever handled a barge pole.

ACKNOWLEDGMENTS

The Woollard End Quanting Society

Punters Everywhere

Those Who Sadly Look Like Barge Poles

Quimbush Merkin

St. Monica's College, Oxford

St. Hubert's College, Cambridge

Lady Estima Davenport

Muriel Dinwiddy

P. L. Chadwick — Rowbarge Pub Image

INTRODUCTION TO BARGE POLES, QUANTS, BOAT HOOKS, AND BARGES

There are presently only a very few barge

pole scholars and perhaps the best know'

during 'The Golden Age of Barge Poles'

were Lady Estima Davenport (1933)

Merkin and Vole eds. **A Brief Account of**

My Quantwork at Oxford (1929-1932)

and Muriel Dinwiddy (1937) Anstruther

and Pules Co. **Tom Puddings, Hopper**

Barges, and Peniches; The Gentlewoman's

Guide to Barge Pole Identification (Revisited).

Further, despite a brief revival of such scholarship as appears in Cormorant, Ralph. B, (2013) Todhunter Press, **Slender Poles and The Working Poleboats of the Mississippi**, Fong, Hirohito, G. (2009) Tojo and Yamamoto Co., **Takasegawa Boating and The Role of The Barge Pole in Choki-Bune Travel** and Frobisher, Dennis (2005) Tolleshunt and D'arcy, **A Guide to Better Quanting When Your Bottom is Shallow and Gravelly**, this slim volume attempts to help navigate the tricky waters of barge-work and trace the exciting history of propelling, fending off objects, and when a barge pole has an attached hook, for holding onto wharfs and jetties.

It is important to begin with some brief conceptual distinctions before proceeding to a history of barges generally and these distinctions involve the differing functions of certain kinds of pole.

A **barge pole** is, for my purposes here, and following Fotheringay E. K (1899) Dalrymple and Dalrymple Press, **An Anthology of Upper-Thames Bargemen**, "a lengthy pole made of wood or metal primarily used by bargemen for **fending** off wharfs, jetties, or other boats and barges." Barge poles must be distinguished from **boat hooks** whose functions are primarily to assist in the activities of **docking and mooring.** Boat hooks may be telescopic or of fixed length, (see Snode and Snode (1968) **Boat Hooks and The Canals of East Anglia.**

Fending Off a Quay or Docking? Barge Pole, Quant, or Boat Hook?

Quants or **quant poles** and **quanting** are terms most commonly associated with the **propulsion** of barges or punts through the water. A **barge quant** often has a cap at the top and a prong at the bottom to stop it from sinking into the mud. In Norfolk,

England these are called a **Bott** and a **Shoe** respectively. A quant used with a punt is about thirteen feet long and made from "either wood or a hollow metal, so that in either case it floats if left in the water." (see Quimmly, Norman (1904) Strabismus Press, **The History of Quants, Botts and Shoes on The Norfolk Broads (Revisited).**

The iconic **Gondola** seems awfully barge or punt-like, since it is a tapered, 32-foot- long flat-bottomed boats historically associated with the canals and lagoon of Venice. Gondolas are propelled from the starboard quarter by a single sweep (oar) manipulated by a gondolier standing on the stern cover, and it has an asymmetrical shape, being 9 inches (23 cm) wider on the port side. A prominent steel beak (ferro) rises from the prow, a lesser one (risso) from the stern. However, the single sweep oar function clearly distinguishes gondola poles from quants, barge poles, and boat hooks even though a gondola pole **can** be used to fend off and also help in mooring and docking, (see, Antonelli, Luigi (1993) Spumante e Barbarossi, **Vedere Quanto è Grande il Mio Palo Gondola è.**

PATIENCE IN A PUNT.

Patience in a Punt Eengraving by W. Dickinson after drawing by H. Bunbury 1791

"Punting, of course is not as easy as it looks. As in rowing, you soon learn how to get along and handle the craft, but it takes long practice before you can do this with dignity and without getting the water all up your sleeve." —Jerome K.

Jerome, Three Men in a Boat (1889).

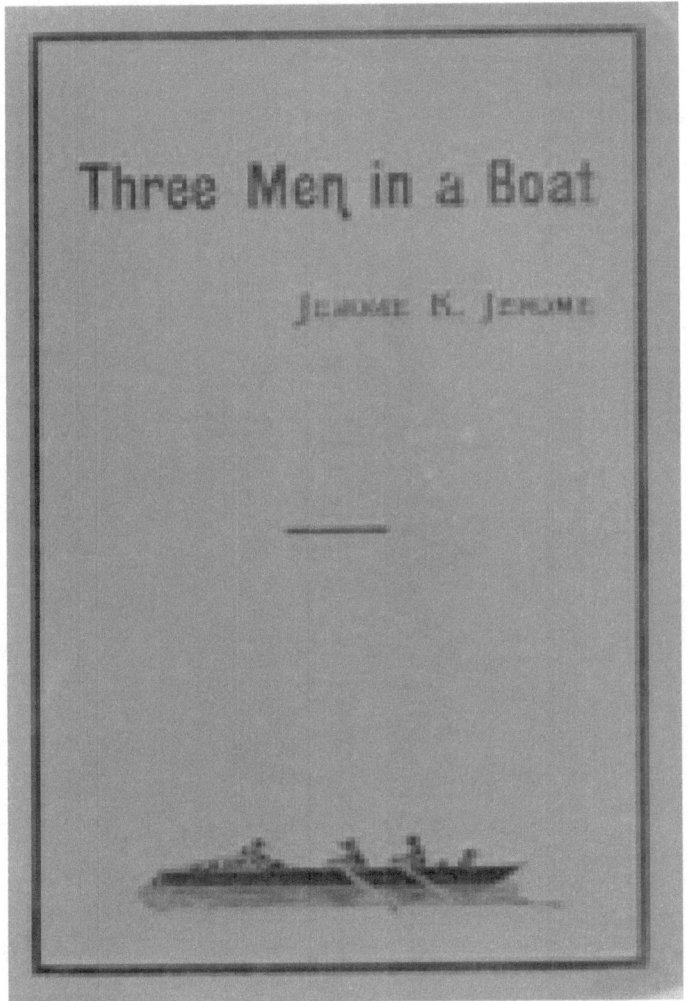

Three Men in a Boat First Edition (1889)

Mr. Briggs and His Doings – John leech

In instructing in the art of punting It has been well-put, " The quanter stands at the front of the barge or, for a punt, normally on the rear deck. The angle at which the quant is held depends on the depth of the water and the desired speed of travel. A steeper angle is required for deeper water (the bottom of the quant must be able to reach the bed of the river or canal) and a shallower angle required for speed. The quanter drives the quant downward and slightly backward to push the craft forwards. On a larger boat, the quanter then walks down the side of the boat, facing aft and braced against the quant pole, the boat being propelled forward at the speed he walks. To reverse, the quant can be pushed forwards. The quant is then pulled out of the water by placing hand over hand on it and pulling upwards (as if one were climbing down a pole)."

A Little Punting (quanting) at Cambridge

The word 'barge', it seems was in common

usage from about from 1300 deriving from the Old French **barge** from turn from the Vulgar Latin *barga.* The word originally could refer to any small boat; the modern meaning of a "flat bottomed vessel 'arose around 1480. Also **bark** a small ship appears in about 1420 from Old French *barque,* from Vulgar Latin *barca* (400 AD). Both are probably derived from the Latin *barica,* via the Greek βάρις.

Cleopatra, it will be recalled from Anthony and Cleopatra had a very fine barge indeed,

Enobarbus: I will tell you.

The barge she sat in, like a burnish'd
throne,
Burned on the water: the poop was beaten
gold;
Purple the sails, and so perfumed that
The winds were lovesick with them; the
oars were silver,
Which to the tune of flutes kept stroke,
and made
The water which they beat to follow
faster,
As amorous of their strokes. For her own
person,
It beggar'd all description: she did lie
In her pavilion, cloth-of-gold of tissue,
O'erpicturing that Venus where we see

The fancy outwork nature: on each side her

Stood pretty dimpled boys, like smiling Cupids,

With divers-colour'd fans, whose wind did seem

To glow the delicate cheeks which they did cool,

And what they undid did. "

The explanation of not touching with a ten foot pole is not commonly agreed upon. The pole concerned is not necessarily a barge pole as in "this expression may have been derived by the 10-foot **pole** electricians and other utility workers use to de-energize transformers and other high voltage utility equipment before performing maintenance".

Also "This expression may have been derived by the 10-foot poles that river boatmen used to **pole** their boats with, along in shallow water, or from the **barge poles** that bargemen used to fend off wharfs and other boats." And further "Many believe this expression originates from a burial practice in New Orleans. The Spanish developed burial system of present day proceeds by first placing the casket of the patron in an above ground tomb. Exactly 1 year and 1 day after burial, the tomb is opened and the casket removed. The body is next wrapped in a sheet and shoved to the back of the tomb with a **ten foot pole** where it falls off the shelf to the bottom. The weather of the area caused the remains to decompose quickly and tombs are subsequently reused for many burial. The expression, "I wouldn't touch it with a **ten foot pole**," is thought to have originated from this burial process." Elsewhere, in the most excellent and scholarly reference work The Phrase Finder the meaning is explained as follows, "(it is) said of something or someone so unappealing that one wouldn't want to go anywhere near. There are various versions of 'I wouldn't touch it with **a pole**, the most commonly used object being either a **barge-pole** or a ten-foot pole. Barge-poles are the long wooden poles used to push barges along. The term was first recorded in Edward Farmer's Scrap book, being a selection of poems, songs, scraps, etc., 1846. The earliest reference I can find to the figurative use of 'wouldn't touch with a **barge-pole**' is Lady Monkswell's Diary, 1893 where it is stated "It will be a long while before any political party touches Home Rule again with the end of a **barge** pole.

The expression appears to derive from the earlier American phrase 'I wouldn't touch that with a **ten-foot pole**'. This is recorded in the magazine of the U.S. Masonic community, *The Official Magazine of the Grand Lodge of the United States*, 1843, edited by James L Ridgely: "But that mushroom aristocracy of our country... who would not condescend to touch a poor man with a **ten foot pole**, were their extraction traced, in nine cases out of ten they were nurtured in the squalid huts of poverty."

Ten-foot poles were, in all likelihood,

barge-poles by another name."

In The Fishing Gazette: Devoted to Angling, River, Lake, and Sea (1896) appears "I never, to my knowledge, saw a barge pole; I know nothing of its size, shape, ... But Mr. Hardy used the word, and in unquestioning confidence I quoted him."

An even earlier use appears in Slick, Jonathan (pseudonym of Ann S. Stephens) High Life in New York (1843) (pp35-36) "A common chap couldn't a touched him with a ten foot pole." Also it is highly derogatory term used to describe an extremely unattractive girl It appears to have originated from the phrase 'I wouldn't touch her with a **bargepole**' as in "you should have seen that bird Keith snogged in the bar last night – she was a total bargepole."

In a recent song by the British hip-hop star Lady Leshur -Lukatar appears the brilliant,

Now hold on a minute, who's this girl though? (Who is she?)
Somebody take this girl home
I dunno why she's giving it the large for
I **wouldn't touch her with a barge pole**
Luktatar, she can't even dress

21

Lady Leshurr, pardon my French

You're not that good and you're hardly
the best
And that squeaky voice, man I'd rather be
deaf
Also in the 19th century traditional folk
song Eggs and Marrowbones appears,

Verse 9

She swam and she swam and she swam
around till she came to the further brim

But the old man got the **barge pole** and he
pushed her further in.

There is always the marvelous mixed
metaphor created by the author, "Trump?
I wouldn't trust him with my **bargepole.**"

Even in *The Christadelphian* appears, "It is in Luke also that there is found the life-sized illustration of each of these men. The Pharisee is Simon (Luke 7:36–50) who invited the Lord to his home, but did not afford him any of the common courtesies of the day. Instead, judging by appearances, he decided that Jesus could not be such a great prophet because he allowed a harlot to touch him, whom Simon **would not touch with a barge-pole!**

Further, the intrepid Henry Morton Stanley, who uttered the immortal words "Dr. Livingstone I presume," now a song by The Moody Blues, also reported some very plucky barge-pole use as in, "However, before I could get near enough to interfere, up rushed a native girl, who, seizing one of these doughty champions in her arms, slung him across her shoulder, as if he had been a baby, and ran away with him. Though so ignominiously borne off, with his head and arms suspended in air, he still brandished his knife, and yelled Ba-Ngala curses at his adversary, who was so overcome by astonishment that he staggered backwards, and sat down in a massanga thus wasting the staple of the evening's entertainment, and being forced to run f or his life to escape the wrath of the disappointed drinkers. It was a plucky feat for a Ba-Ngalawoman,—they usually run away as soon as the knives make their appearance. Had that duskyava old King Mata Bwyki, Lord of Many Guns, been alive, he would have lain about among these brawlers with his **royal barge-pole**, and quickly secured peace and quiet. {Stanley, Henry M. (Henry Morton) A Visit to Stanley's Rear Guard at Major Barttelot's Camp on the Aruhwimi with an Account of River Life on the Congo (Blackwood – Edinburgh (1889)}

Flat bottomed canal boats were very

common in the United States and both England and Holland and were the principal means of the transportation of goods and supplies prior to mechanization and automobiles and trains. This is from a ripping yarn about canal-boat life in Holland.

"The canal boat – so Molly and May packed their trunks, and one day, very soon, Oom Dirks barge sailed up the broad canal close to Oom Jan's windmill. There were many surprises for the Sunbonnet Babies on their uncle's boat. They found that it was his home, and that their Tante Marta and Cousin Bram and the dog Toon lived on it, too. The family was always taking long journeys on the boat. Sometimes they carried a load of cheese or vegetables away over into Germany to sell, and they often brought back a load of stone for building dikes and roads. The barge was a handsome one, with great brown sails that pulled hard in the wind. When there was no wind Bram or his mother or his **father pushed the barge on with a long pole.** And so they traveled, sailing and poling all summer—and all winter, too, when the canals were not frozen. The Sunbonnet Babies were delighted with the strange, floating house.

We must see every corner of it, Molly's aid.

You must show us everything, Bram. All

right, said B." {**The Sunbonnet Babies in**

Holland – **A Second Reader** (1915)

Grover, Eulalie Osgood (1873) Rand

McNally and Company.}

A Flat-Bottomed Dutch Canal Barge
Poling Along in the 1800s

And again, "The barge was almost as long

as the Sun-bonnet Babies house in America, but it was very low and narrow. The load of rocks or vegetables was carried in the front half of the barge, while the family lived in the back part. At first Molly and May thought there would not be much room for play, but when Bram showed them all his games they were sure his barge was the finest playground in the world. Bram's dog Toon could do all sorts of queer tricks. The children had great fun running races and playing tag with him. But flying kites was the most fun. Bram made a handsome kite for each of the Sunbonnet Babies. On May's kite he painted a big flying bluebird, and on Molly's kite he painted a long-legged stork.

Here's a fine gale of wind for our kites, Bram said one morning. See how fast the big sails are pulling our barge along. We shall have no poling to do to-day. So they let out their kites into the wind".

"No barge poling today!"

So far we have seen that the distinctions among the various types of poles that have been mentioned are largely a matter of use and the same functions can be accomplished interchangeably since a ten to thirteen foot pole is a terribly useful implement.

The Delightful Rowbarge Pub, Guildford, England where the Author frequently Moistened while in Law School

Ohio River Barges in 1907

Barges were vital to large scale
transportation in the 19th Century in the
United States. Accounts include, "Settlers
wanted to carry their families, household
furniture, tools, grain, and all the
produce of the land, they needed
something larger and stronger. At first
they built barges, which were little more
than great boxes made water-tight. These

they loaded and steered down the stream as best they could. They did not expect to bring hem back, for such boats could not be pushed against the current. Hence the barge builders at Pittsburg always had work, for a new one had to be provided for each fresh cargo. Later men began to make keel boats, in which they could not only go downstream but could also, **by poling**, make a return voyage. These boats were about fifty feet long and could carry twenty tons or more. Along the sides were running boards, where the men went up and down with their setting poles to drive the boat against the current."

{Bringham, Albert Perry, **Description and Travel Ohio River Valley**, Ginn and Company, Boston and New York (1907}

Using a Barge Pole to Dock (Left)

We can find an excellent example of a barge pole assisting in docking in Johann Barthold Jonkind Dutch (1819-1891) — Dutch Canal by Moonlight. The text states

"Against the luminosity of the moonlit sky a windmill rises darkly on the right bank of the canal. In the shadow beneath it a barge is being brought to its mooring by two men, one of whom hauls on a rope while the other **pushes with a pole**. In the center of the stream, a boat with its sail down is being **poled along** by two men. It is moving in the direction of a tall, arched bridge, supported on three piers, behind which are dimly visible another windmill and some trees."

In the Indian sub-continent where many hundreds of millions of people are daily waterborne we can find flat bottomed barges poling along waterways and docked

using barge poles of various kinds.

Local Fellow with a Boat Hook Awaiting
the Arrival of the 4.30 from Mar Nalla
Junction (1912)

{Neve, Ernest Frederick, Beyond the Pir

Panjal; Life Among the Mountains and

Valleys of Kashmir (1912) Roberts, Toronto 1912.

"There is often a large house-boat, of European pattern, with windows and upper-deck, comes steadily down-stream, carefully steered by men with large paddles and long punting poles.

The banks in many places are lined with great barge-like boats laden with stones, earth, hay, rice and many othercargoes. Where there is space on the sandy shore, lines of logs are moored and sawyers are busily at work with their double hand-saw, one standing on the beam, which is tilted up at an angle, and the other beneath.

Many of the houses which line the banks are built on stone foundations, among which are numerous carved frag-ments from demolished temples.

In places, these walls are pierced by doorways leading to the water's edge.

Above are balconies built out and resting on timber pillars or brackets. Some have windows of lattice work, beautifully pieced together.

Here and there between the houses are alleys or lanes which open on to the river."

Catching a Mermaid (1883)

One of the most useful attributes of barge

pole like boat hooks is recovering

mermaids. Here in the previous

engaging work **Catching a Mermaid**

(1883) by the wonderfully named

James Clarke Hook (1819-1907)

"Two boys and a girl are portrayed on rocks at the water's edge. The narrative indicates that they have discovered a wrecked ship's figurehead and, armed with ropes and a **boat-hook**, attempt to haul it ashore. **boat-hook**. The girl restrains the younger boy, while the older boy perches near the edge of the rocks and secures the figurehead with a rope."

Boat hooks and poles regularly appear in heraldry as the following will attest.

The Arms of Wappen

DEU Seelow

Coat of Arms of Nexo. Svg

Wappen Landkreis Oder-Spree

It will have been seen in this slim volume

that barges and barge poles have been used in aquatic transport for several thousand years. It will also have been seen that various long poles have multiple functions for propelling, repelling, docking, and that their names are commonly used interchangeably such that function is use.

Finally it should be noted "On the British Canal system, (with which the author is familiar) the term 'barge' is used to describe a boat wider than a narrow boat and the people who move barges are often known as lighterman. In the United States, deckhands perform the labor and are supervised by a leadsman or the mate. The captain and pilot steer the towboat, which pushes one or more barges held together with rigging, collectively called 'the tow'. The crews live aboard the towboat as it travels along the inland river system or the intracoastal waterways. These towboats travel between ports and are also called line-haul boats. **Poles** are used on barges to fend off the barge as it nears other vessels or a wharf. These are often called **'pike poles'**." Happy quanting to you all!

Keith Pepperell

ABOUT THEAUTHOR

The author lives in the green bean casserole belt of the mid – west and might be slightly mad

Keith Pepperell

www.ingramcontent.com/pod-product-compliance
Lightning Source LLC
Chambersburg PA
CBHW030539290526
45786CB00004B/1785